A Walk Through Our Garden

Asa E. Low Jr.

Bedford, Texas

Dedication

This book is dedicated to my wonderful wife of fifty-six years, Linda G. Low. She is a spiritual giant, a prayer -warrior, and an encourager, who is dedicated to her Lord Jesus Christ and to her husband. We have walked our life together depending on the Lord's mercy, grace, provision, and each other. She was my inspiration for starting a flower garden in the first place. After she had brain surgery in 2000 to remove a tumor, I wanted Linda to have something peaceful and beautiful to see; so, I began planting flowers. I love her with all my being!

I have learned much from the Lord and His creation, and I hope that these devotionals reveal God's love for humanity.

Acknowledgments

I thank my wonderful family for their prayers and encouragement: my wife, Linda, who inspired the beginning of planting a garden; our daughter, Ambre Alston; our son, Asa E. Low, III and his wife, Jennifer; our son Aaron David Low and his wife Veronica, who encouraged me to publish this book, my son Andrew Michael Low and his wife Brandy, who encouraged me to write.

I would also like to thank my grandchildren Kaitlyn Low, Asa E. Low, IV, Julianna Low, Symphony Low, Nathan Alston, Nadia Low, and Vivienne Low, for whom I wrote the book.

Much thanks go to my former student, Matt Manire for his encouragement and my dear friend Bob Denton who always believes in me.

Most of all, I want to thank my Lord and Savior, Jesus Christ, who gives me strength each day.

Contents

Foreword

Asa Low has been my friend, mentor, and pastor since 1982. The words and photos he shares in this wonderful book are going to allow you and your loved ones to clearly see the direct connection between God's magnificent creation and His endless love for us. I would recommend that you read this book slowly and deliberately .... letting every word and image sink deep into your heart!

Romans 1:20

For ever since the world was created, people have seen the earth and sky. Through everything God made, they can clearly see His invisible qualities—
His eternal power and divine nature.

Bob Denton
Care Pastor
Turning Point Church
Fort Worth, TX
wwwtpcfamily.org

A Walk Through Our Garden:

Esperanza means HOPE

The striking, tubular two and one-half-inch bright yellow flowers are highlighted by the attractive, shiny, green foliage and continue through the heat of the summer. The flowers have an odd but pleasing fragrance and also provide nectar for bees. The Indians made bows from its wood (It is hard for me to believe.), and in Mexico a beer was prepared from its roots; it has also been used for a variety of medicines (Wikipedia).

Photo by Linda

Psalm 119

49 Remember your promise to me; it is my only hope.
81 I am worn out waiting for your rescue, but I have put my hope in your word.
114 You are my refuge and my shield; your word is my source of hope.

Esperanza is a Spanish word which means hope. We have two beautiful plants which die down each year. I cut the canes even with the ground, and the beauties return every year averaging a height of 6 feet.

I am reminded in Proverbs 13:12 that "Hope deferred makes the heart sick, but a dream fulfilled is a tree of life."

I have noticed that when people lose their hope, their complete world is turned upside down and inside out. A person may become extremely quiet, reclusive, or irritable, depressed, or even suicidal. It is so important for us to encourage ourselves in the Lord through the scriptures, prayer, praise, and worship; however, when our hope diminishes to extinction, we need the encouragement of a real live person who can remind us of what Jesus has done, what He can do, and remind us that God has a plan for our future regardless of our age.

Please encourage someone today! Speak to them! Write a note! Share a scripture! "Rescue the perishing. Care for the dying." Grow an esperanza plant to remind yourself of God's hope for you!!!

Blessings, and praise God from whom all blessings flow!!!

God's Creativity in Our Garden

Plumbago

Psalm 8:1-4, 9

1 O Lord, our Lord, your majestic name fills the earth!
Your glory is higher than the heavens.
2 You have taught children and infants
to tell of your strength, silencing your enemies and all who oppose you.
3 When I look at the night sky and see the work of your fingers—
the moon and the stars you set in place—
4 what are mere mortals that you should think about them,
human beings that you should care for them?
9 O Lord, our Lord, your majestic name fills the earth!

Photo by Linda

The flowers of the Plumbago come in a variety of colors—white, blue, purple, red, or pink, with a tubular corolla with five petal-like lobes. The plant is usually 1.6 feet-6 feet tall. The outer most part of the flower has glandular hairs, which secrete a sticky mucilage that is capable of trapping and killing insects. It is unclear what the purpose of these hairs might be; protection from pollination by way of "crawlers" (ants and other insects that typically do not transfer pollen between individual plants), or possible protocarnivory (Wikipedia).

Is not God's creativity amazing? Our Plumbago is a soft powdery blue, likes the heat, and is a bushy perennial. You will not find insects on this plant unless the plant is about to eat them!

When I view God's creation, I am astounded. Can you imagine that if God is so intricate with animals and plants, how much more is He concerned with your life, your plan, your purpose. Seek the Lord today in all that you do!

Blessings, and praise God from whom all blessings flow!

God Uses the Wanderer

Wandering Purple Jew

Revelation 4:11

You are worthy, O Lord our God, to receive glory and honor and power. For you created all things, and they exist because you created what you pleased.

The Purple Heart Plant or Wondering-purple Jew is easy to root, enjoys indirect sun light, and has dark, beautiful, purple colored leaves with a teeny, tiny, light purple flower. Our plants this year are more beautiful than this previous year's picture. Over the years, I have taken cuttings from this plant and made many hanging baskets.

Photo by Linda

When I view our beautiful plants, I am reminded of the redemptive, gracious, loving, benevolent heart of God the Father, Son, and Holy Spirit. I begin to be so grateful for the enduring love, mercy, and grace that God has given to me. Life is not without storms, disappointments, losses, and challenges; nevertheless, I am, and have been so marvelously blessed! I cannot praise Him enough!

Blessings, and praise God from whom all blessings flow!

Purslane

Cultivated Purslane is an annual succulent in the family which contains 40 varieties that are currently cultivated. It has culinary and medicinal uses. (Wikipedia) I do not think that I will eat any of our plants, but Linda might.

Photo by Linda

The flowers on our plants are yellow, orange, hot pink, pink, white, purple and red. Bees love to crawl down into the blooms and wallow around in them. Linda and I will never forget when Kaitlyn, our oldest grandchild, was about three years old. She saw a bee crawling into a bloom. She reached out and gently closed the petals around the bee with her fingers. Then, she turned loose, and the bee flew out and continued buzzing from flower to flower, not in the least disturbed. Ah, the wonder of childhood discovery, before they become afraid of what they do not understand.

God is just like that flower. He offers us the sweet nectar of His word that we may thrive and gather wisdom, guidance, direction, counsel, and comfort. A life without Christ and accountability is one who wanders—like a sailing ship without a sail, rudder, or engine—who lives selfishly for himself and is never satisfied. As we are dependent on Him, we, like the bee, focused on its purpose, will live, realize our destiny and purpose in Christ, and love, honor, serve, and prefer others!

Blessings, and praise God from whom all blessings flow!

Praise the Lord!

Salvia

Psalm 148:13 NLT

Let them all praise the name of the Lord.
For his name is very great; his glory towers over the earth and heaven!

Photo by Brandy Low

Our "Mystic Spires" Blue Salvia produces masses of true blue flowers that mix nicely with other annuals and perennials. It is tolerant of heat and humidity both low and high humidity. It is not bothered by pests or diseases, and it loves full sun. Salvia is a perennial which dies down and grows back every year to a height between 12 and 30 inches tall. (Wikipedia).

I love the way the bees and butterflies come to this plant. I am reminded of majestic praise to the Lord—tall, erect, and unencumbered. May I share this dear hymn?

"For the beauty of the earth, For the glory of the skies,
For the love which from our birth Over and around us lies;
Christ our God, to Thee we raise
This our hymn of grateful praise.

"For the wonder of each hour of the day and of the night,
Hill and vale, and tree and flower, Sun and moon, and stars of light;
Christ our God, to Thee we raise
This our hymn of grateful praise.

"For the joy of human love, Brother, sister, parent, child,
Friends on earth, and friends above, For all gentle thought and mild;
Christ our God, to Thee we raise
This our hymn of grateful praise.

"For Thy Church that evermore
Lifteth holy hands above, Offering up on every shore
Her pure sacrifice of love;
Christ our God, to Thee we raise
This our hymn of grateful praise."
(Selah—pause and meditate)

Pierpont/Kocher

Blessings, and praise God from whom all blessings flow!

Be Strong and Courageous

Pentas

Psalm 145:1-3 NLT

1 I will exalt you, my God and King, and praise your name forever and ever.
2 I will praise you every day; yes, I will praise you forever.
3 Great is the Lord! He is most worthy of praise!
No one can measure his greatness.

Our Butterfly Red, Purple, and White Pentas are tolerant to high heat, various soils, and pests. They are low maintenance and provide a profusion of bright red blooms from spring to frost. They need full sun to partial shade, and can grow to 24 inches tall and 24 inches wide (Wikipedia).

Photo by Linda Low

Pentas remind me of God's word that produces strength, stamina, and courage that yields endurance in the midst of life's storms—losses, tragedies, and disappointments. "Be strong and of good courage …!"

When you are facing a tremendous life storm and you have been in the scriptures, prayed, praised, and worshipped until you are blue in the face, do the following:

1. Believe the promise and plan of God,
2. Be strong and be willing to make the effort to know God, and
3. Be courageous—face your fears, and do what is right.

Do not move unnecessarily just to fulfill your anxiety, BUT move through doors that God opens—and He will open those doors!

Blessings, and praise God from whom all blessings flow!

A Cure for Depression: Calibrachoa

Nehemiah 8:10b

…Do not be dejected and sad, for the joy of the Lord is your strength!

We have had the calibrachoa or million bells plant for several years. I just love this plant. It is so joyful and happy that you can almost hear it sing.

Photo by Linda

Calibrachoa also known as "million bells" has flowers that look like bells. It overflows the hanging basket, continually blooms all summer, and takes full to partial sun. It can grow up and in between other plants, but in full shade it will stretch and look long and spindly (Wikipedia).

> "Praise to the Lord, the Almighty, the King of creation!
> O my soul, praise Him, for He is thy health and salvation!
> All ye who hear, now to His temple draw near;
> Praise Him in glad adoration!"
>
> Joachim Neander

Praise drives away depression, doubt, fear, and oppression. Stay in the sun (Son), otherwise the darkness of the shade (depression) will stretch you and make you sad or reclusive (spindly) and of no encouragement or service to others.

Blessings, and praise God from whom all blessings flow!

Behold the Lilies of the Field

Day Lily

Revelation 4:11

You are worthy, O Lord,
To receive glory and honor and power;
For You created all things,
And by Your will they exist and were created.

Daylilies are perennial plants that open in early morning and wither during the following night, possibly to be replaced by another one on the same flower stalk the next day. The plants are native to Asia, primarily eastern Asia, including China, Korea, and Japan. This genus is popular worldwide because of the showy flowers and hardiness (Wikipedia).

Photo by Brandy Low

We have several clumps of these beauties which originally belonged to my mother. These flowers show forth such majesty and illustrate the glory and honor that we should demonstrate in worship to our Creator—HIS MAJESTY—JESUS!!!

Acts 17:28a

For in him we live and move and exist.

Blessings, and praise God from whom all blessings flow!

He Rejoices Over Us!

Japanese Aralia

Isaiah 43:1b-3a NLT

1 Do not be afraid, for I have ransomed you.
I have called you by name; you are mine.
2 When you go through deep waters, I will be with you.
When you go through rivers of difficulty, you will not drown.
When you walk through the fire of oppression, you will not be burned up;
the flames will not consume you.
3 For I am the Lord, your God, the Holy One of Israel, your Savior.
(Selah moment)

The Japanese Aralia portrays long, upright leaf stems that hold glossy, lobed leaves with pointed tips. Each leaf has between 7–9 inch lobes and can reach up to 12 in (30 cm) across. This fast-growing, evergreen shrub is an easy care. It seems to shrug off pests and diseases, and it needs little attention to thrive. You can keep it happy by watering regularly and providing good drainage. Overwatering can cause root rot. You can move it outdoors in the summer if you want. Just be sure to put it in a shaded spot, because direct sun can burn its leaves.

This plant needs a rest in winter. Move it to a cool spot where the temperature doesn't dip below 45°F/7°C and water less frequently. (Wikipedia) The pictured plants thrived for 15 years; however, the extreme freeze of near zero in February, 2021 and December of 2022 killed our four plants. I had to replant.

Photos by Linda

Scriptural parallel: I purchased the plant. I prayed and sang over it during extreme hot and cold temperatures. I dug around them, watered, and fertilized them.

The Lord is our Master Gardener. He knows us! "He rejoices over us with singing." He purchased us, protects us, prunes us, and nurtures us. He gives us the water and food of His holy scriptures—and rejoices over our prayers, praise, and worship!!

When we face difficulties (storms), He is with us! We will not drown, nor be consumed by fire because He is the Lord of Lords and King of Kings and has a plan and purpose for our lives!!!

17 … our God whom we serve is able to deliver us from the burning fiery furnace, and He will deliver us from your hand, O king. 18 But if not, let it be known to you, O king, that we do not serve your gods, nor will we worship the gold image which you have set up. (Daniel 3:17-18)

Blessings, and praise God from whom all blessings flow!

Trust and Obey the Lord

Boston Fern

Proverbs 3:5-6 NLT

*5 Trust in the Lord with all your heart; do not depend
on your own understanding. 6 Seek his will in all you do,
and he will show you which path to take.*

The Boston Fern's fronds rise from an upright, underground rhizome. Each long, arching frond can grow to 4-6 feet in length and is divided into many narrow pinnae growing alternately on either side of the midrib. Each pinna is itself cut into a number of segments, giving the plants a feathery appearance (Wikipedia).

We have six Boston Ferns that are beautiful, but not as large as the description portrays.

Photo by Linda

This frilly, happy plant that loves indirect light reminds me of one who just blindly and joyfully trusts the Lord and does not try to reason every minute detail of life. This person seeks, trusts, and obeys the Lord fully for guidance and direction.

Meditate on the following hymn.

"When we walk with the Lord in the Light of His Word
What a glory He sheds on our way!
While we do His good will, He abides with us still,
And with all who will trust and obey.

"Not a burden we bear, not a sorrow we share,
But our toil He doth richly repay;
Not a grief nor a loss, not a frown or a cross,
But is blest if we trust and obey.

"But we never can prove the delights of His love
Until all on the altar we lay;
For the favor He shows, and the joy He bestows,
Never fear, only trust and obey.

Chorus:

"Trust and obey, for there's no other way to be happy in Jesus,
But to trust and obey."

Sammis/Towner

Blessings, and praise God from whom all blessings flow!

God Has a Plan for You

Fig Tree

Isaiah 54:2 NKJ

Enlarge the place of your tent,
And let them stretch out the curtains of your dwellings;
Do not spare;
Lengthen your cords,
And strengthen your stakes.

The fig is a picturesque deciduous tree, growing up to 50 feet tall, but more typically to a height of 10–30 feet. The branches are muscular and twisting, spreading wider than they are tall. Fig wood is weak and decays rapidly. ("We are weak, but He is strong!") Fig leaves are bright green, single, and large (to 1 foot length). The tiny flowers of the fig are out of sight, clustered inside the green "fruits". (We are in the palm of His hand!) The matured "fruit" has a tough peel (Wikipedia).

Be mature in the Lord—tough to temptations, slow to speak, quick to listen, and rapid to obey.

Photo by Linda

Our beautiful fig tree was about 20 feet tall and a bushy 10 feet wide. The terrible February of 2021 freeze killed the branches. Therefore, I cut it to the ground. It came back from the roots and is now about 6 feet tall and 10 feet wide.

The fig tree is symbolic of Israel. There is much that I could share; however, think about the above description in a spiritual sense. The country of Israel was re-established in 1948, and it has had opposition before and has ever since.

As a Christian, not everyone will like or love you; nevertheless, tomorrow is a time of new beginnings. Regardless of your age, God still has a plan and purpose for your life. Begin to dream in a new direction! Expand your thoughts! "Lengthen your cords and strengthen your stakes." Do not fear opposition!

If God has given you the dream, give Him permission to accomplish it, and quit limiting Him! "Enlarge!" Stretch out!" "Lengthen!" "Strengthen!" Do not sit on the dream, but MOVE in God's direction by His Word, prayer, praise, worship, and accountability! The time for new beginnings is now! Are you listening to me? The time is now!

Blessings, and praise God from whom all blessings flow!

Reminder to Praise

Zinnias

Luke 19:37-40 NKJV

37 Then, as He was now drawing near the descent of the Mount of Olives, the whole multitude of the disciples began to rejoice and praise God with a loud voice for all the mighty works they had seen, 38 saying: "'Blessed is the King who comes in the name of the LORD!' Peace in heaven and glory in the highest!" 39 And some of the Pharisees called to Him from the crowd, "Teacher, rebuke your disciples." 40 But He answered and said to them, "I tell you that if these should keep silent, the stones would immediately cry out."

Photo by Linda

Zinnia is a genus of 20 species of annual and perennial plants in an area stretching from the American Southwest to South America, but primarily Mexico, and notable for their solitary long-stemmed flowers that come in a variety of bright colors—white, chartreuse, yellow, orange, red, purple, and lilac. Zinnias are popular garden flowers, usually grown from seed, and preferably in fertile, humus-rich, and well-drained soil, in an area with full sun. Its leaves are lance-shaped and sandpapery in texture, and its height ranges from 7 inches to 40 inches. Zinnias seem especially favored by butterflies (Wikipedia).

The zinnia is a joyful plant that gives us great color and reminds me of the praise in the above passage. Praise to the Lord our God may sound like a religious activity that is worthless; however, when you have had a near death experience, or have been healed from some dread disease, or you've received financial, emotional, and physical rescue from the Lord, your attitude turns to uncontrollable gratitude.

In November of 2018, our oldest grandson, Asa IV, and my wife, Linda, were both diagnosed with cancer. Five months later our son, Aaron, was in a horrible auto accident. It was almost more than I could endure emotionally; HOWEVER, GOD—by HIS WORD has HEALED them ALL.

Our grandson Asa IV has had a great five year report. He graduated from Navarro College with an Associate's Degree in May 2023 and graduated from high school 4 weeks later. He entered Texas Tech in the fall of 2023 as a junior.

Linda has had a great five-year report.

Aaron's leg fractures have mostly healed; AND, He is alive, well, and working!

God's WORD is SO important!!! It has sustained us through it all! Who can praise our God enough? "Praise to the Lord, the Almighty, the King of creation!" Take time to praise the Lord today!

Blessings, and praise God from whom all blessings flow!

The Sweetness of His Word

Butterfly Bush

Psalm 34:1 NLT

I will praise the Lord at all times. I will constantly speak his praises.

The Buddleia Butterfly Bush contains large, fragrant flower clusters up to 15" long. They emit a delicate scent that attracts butterflies and hummingbirds to your garden. Bright pink (or purple) blooms display gorgeous color from summer to fall. The plant grows 6-10' tall with similar spread (Wikipedia).

Photo by Linda

When I gaze on our beautiful Buddleia Butterfly Bush, I am reminded of sweet times that we, as needy people desperate to hear and know God, meditate on scripture, pray, praise, and worship our God. Either in private or corporate worship, with reckless abandon, we sing loudly, raise our hands, and dance before the Lord.

Have you noticed (spiritually) that when we praise and worship our God, a fragrant aroma is being presented to our God, and His presence is attracted back to us.

Blessings, and praise God from whom all blessings flow!

Each One of Us is His Special Creation

Mandevilla

Psalm 8:1 AMP

O LORD, our Lord, how excellent [majestic and glorious] is Your name in all the earth! You have set Your glory on [or above] the heavens.

Photos by Linda Low

In 2020, we had five Mandevillas, pink, yellow, and red. In 2021, we had four plants which were red and pink. In 2022 and 2023, we had only three red plants. They are extremely beautiful, love the heat, but need watering two times daily.

We are beautiful creations of God. We are "wonderfully made" in all shapes, colors, and sizes. We must have daily watering from God's scriptures, or we will wither and die. God is our Creator, and He desires to have a relationship with us. Our daily concerns become opportunities for panic to set in and change our direction.

Take time today to listen, put electronic devices away for a few minutes, gaze on the beauty of creation, listen to your Creator, and be amazed at the intricacies of His creation.

Psalm 46:10 NLT

Be still, and know that I am God! I will be honored by every nation.
I will be honored throughout the world.

Blessings, and praise God from whom all blessings flow!

Our Heritage in the Lord

Swedish Ivy

Psalm 16: 5-6

5 O Lord, You are the portion of my inheritance and my cup;
You maintain my lot.
6 The lines have fallen to me in pleasant places;
Yes, I have a good inheritance.

Psalm 100:1

Make a joyful shout to the Lord, all you lands!

Photo by Linda

Red Swedish ivy is a misnomer, as this delightful vining plant is neither Swedish in origin, nor is it a true ivy, nor is it completely red—but has a red tint underneath the leaf. However, Swedish Ivy plants did originally become popular as a house plant in Sweden. Native to Africa and Australia, Swedish ivy thrives in bright light and high humidity but is not overly sensitive to normal household conditions. As a vining plant, it makes an attractive hanging basket with its shiny green leaves with scalloped edges (Nannette Richford—*Home and Produce Magazine*).

This plant gives us great joy and reminds us of the great spiritual heritage from which we have benefited. When your mother and father are strong in their faith in Jesus, you reap the rewards of that spiritual blessing. I can say with the psalmist "You are the portion of my inheritance and my cup; You maintain my lot."

Blessings, and praise God from whom all blessings flow!

A Sweet-smelling Aroma

Dianthus Barbatus

Psalm 141:2

Let my prayer be set before You as incense,
The lifting up of my hands as the evening sacrifice.

Ephesians 5:2

And walk in love, as Christ also has loved us and given Himself for us,
an offering and a sacrifice to God for a sweet-smelling aroma.

Photo by Linda

Dianthus barbatus, commonly known as Sweet William, produces flowers in shades of white, red, pink, and variations of those colors. Sweet William can reach up to 18 inches in height. The Dianthus barbatus is suited to cool areas and the flowers do not grow well in tropical locations. Sweet William flowers fill the garden with a sweet and spice-like fragrance. (Wikipedia).

Our Sweet William plants have a prominent place near our fountain. This beautiful plant attracts butterflies. Our plant has endured extreme hot and cold temperatures and just keeps blooming.

As Christ followers, it is so important that our actions demonstrate the sweet fragrance of our Lord throughout difficult times. I still like to ask myself daily—"What would Jesus do? How would Jesus react?"

Prayer

Dear Lord, please guard my mouth from uttering stupid words, and You cleanse my heart and mouth oh, Lord. Let me be sensitive to Your Holy Spirit. Please help me demonstrate your love and kindness to others. Let me demonstrate your sweet fragrance.
In Jesus' name. Amen.

Blessings, and praise God from whom all blessings flow!

Show Forth the Peace of God

Scaevola

Isaiah 52:7

How beautiful on the mountains are the feet of the messenger who brings good news, the good news of peace and salvation, the news that the God of Israel reigns!

Scaevola is a genus of flowering plants in the Goodenia family, Goodeniaceae. It consists of more than 130 tropical species, with the center of diversity being Australia and Polynesia. Common names for Scaevola species include scaevolas, fan-flowers, half-flowers, and naupaka, the plants' Hawaiian name. The flowers are shaped as if they have been cut in half. Consequently, the generic name means "left-handed" in Latin. (Wikipedia)

Photo by Linda

The above verse Isaiah 52:7 was the first verse to come to mind when I think how awesome our God is and what our responsibility is to share the good news of Jesus who loves the world. Linda and I want our home to be a place of peace, a retreat and refuge from a busy world, a place that exemplifies "the news that the God of Israel reigns!"

It is so easy to be distracted from what God wants you to do by all that is going on in the world and in our country. Please do not focus your time on people or politicians you like or do not like. Focus on God's purpose for your life. What would Jesus do and how would He act?

Prayer

Jesus, teach us to love one another as you gave your life for us.
In Jesus' name, Amen.

Blessings, and praise God from whom all blessings flow!

God Created You for Purpose

Hibiscus

Psalm 96:12

Let the field be joyful, and all that is in it.
Then all the trees of the woods will rejoice before the Lord.

Psalm 66: 1-2

1 Make a joyful shout to God, all the earth!
2 Sing out the honor of His name;
Make His praise glorious.

Hardy Hibiscus   Double Hibiscus

Photos by Linda

Tropical Hibiscus

The hibiscus is a beautiful flowering plant and ranges from about 12 inches to four plus feet—containing several hundred species that are native to warm-temperate, subtropical and tropical regions throughout the world. Many species are grown for their showy flowers or used as landscape shrubs, and are used to attract butterflies, bees, and hummingbirds. The hibiscus can be used for making paper, hot or cold tea, or as an edible delicacy. It is the national flower of South Korea, Malaysia, Haiti, the state flower of Hawaii, and it is traditionally worn by Tahitian and Hawaiian girls.(Wikipedia).

Life Application:

We have several beautiful hibiscus—red, pink, yellow, and peach. Each plant has many flowers which only last for one day; but, more come daily. They shout their praise to the Lord and to all who take time to watch!

"Praise to the Lord the Almighty, the King of Creation!"

Take time to really look at the intricacies of colors and design—the petals, stem, pistil, stamen, and leaves. God is such an intricate designer and planner! Since God has given so much detail to plants, how much more to us!

He loves us with an everlasting love and offers a plan, purpose, provision, and direction for our life. Take time to consume the scriptures and talk to our creator today. He loves you so much that He can't take His eyes off of you!

Blessings, and praise God from whom all blessings flow!

God's Love and Provision

Canna Lily

Psalm 8:1

O Lord, our Lord,
How excellent is Your name in all the earth,
Who have set Your glory above the heavens!

Canna (or canna lily, although not a true lily) is a genus of 10 species of flowering plants. The plants have large foliage and horticulturists have turned it into a large-flowered garden plant. It is also used in agriculture as a rich source of starch for human and animal consumption.

Although a plant of the tropics, most cultivars have been developed in temperate climates and are easy to grow in most countries of the world as long as they receive at least 6–8 hours average daily sunlight during the summer (Wikipedia).

Photo by Linda

As we gaze upon our beautiful plants, I am reminded of the majesty and splendor of our God.

John 3:16-17

For God so loved the world that He gave His only begotten Son,
that whoever believes in Him should not perish but have everlasting life.
For God did not send His Son into the world to condemn the world,
but that the world through Him might be saved.

God is all about loving us and providing for us, not condemning us.

"Trust and obey, for there is no other way to be happy in Jesus."
J.H. Sammis/D. B. Towner

Blessings, and praise God from whom all blessings flow!

Dahlia

Psalm 32:11

So rejoice in the Lord and be glad, all you who obey him! Shout for joy,
all you whose hearts are pure!

The dahlia stems are leafy, ranging in height from as low as 12 inches to more than 6–8 feet. The majority of species do not produce scented flowers. Like most plants that do not attract pollinating insects through scent, they are brightly colored, displaying most color hues, with the exception of blue. The dahlia was declared the national flower of Mexico in 1963. The tubers were grown as a food crop by the Aztecs, but this use largely died out after the Spanish Conquest. Attempts to introduce the tubers as a food crop in Europe were unsuccessful (Wikipedia).

Photo by Linda

Our dahlias are red, yellow, orange, and purple. This flower reminds me of the above verse. We have a choice each day to be glad or mad, to be happy or sad, to be grateful and thankful OR to be selfish, unhappy, and self-centered.

What is God calling you to do today? Are you thinking about how to honor, serve, and prefer others; or are you bogged down thinking of your own desires and stresses? We have a choice today to be glad, happy, and obedient to our God! Yea! If you are stressed by the cares you are facing, try praising the Lord. It will lift your spirit and fill you with joy!

Blessings, and praise God from whom all blessings flow!

The Beautiful Fragrance of Christian Love

Iris

Proverbs 27:9

The heartfelt counsel of a friend is as sweet as perfume and incense.

Proverbs 17:7

A friend is always loyal, and a brother is born to help in time of need.

Photos by Linda

Iris is a genus of 260 species of flowering plants with showy flowers (Wikipedia).

Our irises usually start blooming in cool February and end in mid to late May. Their beauty is overwhelming, and their fragrance will give you a life's selah (pause/think) moment. The iris reminds me of the above verses and 1 Corinthians 13. It is my prayer and wish for you that you have a Christian friend—but especially a spouse with whom you can speak, get counsel, share the wonders, beauties, sadness, regrets, and frustrations of life in confidence.

Our marriage of 56 years (in March of 2023) is one that contains the following qualities: commitment to God and to each other, friendship (she is my best friend), patience, kindness, not envious, not proud or boastful, not rude, thinks the best of each other, not jealous, thinks no evil, rejoices in the truth; and, finally, is built on continually learning how to honor, serve, and prefer each other. The fragrance of that relationship is overwhelming to me.

Blessings, and praise God from whom all blessings flow!

God Causes Us to Thrive

Morning Glory

John 3: 16-17

*For God so loved the world that He gave His only begotten Son,
that whoever believes in Him should not perish but have everlasting life.
For God did not send His Son into the world to condemn the world,
but that the world through Him might be saved.*

The Morning glory is the common name for over 1,000 species of flowering plants. Most morning glory flowers unravel into full bloom in the early morning. The flowers usually start to fade a few hours before the petals start showing visible curling. Morning glories prefer full sun; however, some morning glories, are night-blooming flowers. Because of their fast growth, twining habit, attractive flowers, and tolerance for poor, dry soils, some morning glories are excellent vines for creating summer shade (Wikipedia).

Photo by Linda

Life Application:

I am totally amazed at the beauty of this plant. One of our granddaughters, Symphony, planted mixed seed colors; and, now, her beautiful flowering plant has outgrown the trellis and is intertwined on a fence. God demonstrates his love to us daily.

When I look at our garden, I reflect on the goodness, kindness, patience, provision, beauty, and faithfulness of our God. God sees the beauty of our potential and takes our poor, dry soil (our self-will) and twining habits (our rebellious nature), and not only causes us to grow, but to thrive! Our responsibility is to surrender our complete spirit, soul, and body to the Master Gardener's hands.

> "And when I think that God, His Son,
> not sparing, sent Him to die,
> I scarce can take it in;
> "That on the cross, my burden gladly bearing,
> He bled and died to take away my sin.
>
> "Then sings my soul, my Savior God, to Thee;
> How great Thou art! How great Thou art!
> Then sings my soul, my Savior God to Thee;
> How great Thou art! How great Thou art!"
>
> Stuart K. Hine

Blessings, and praise God from whom all blessings flow!

Lollipop Plant

Isaiah 60: 1

Arise, shine; For your light has come!
And the glory of the Lord is risen upon you.

Revelation 7:11-13

All the angels stood around the throne and the elders and the four living
creatures, and fell on their faces before the throne and worshiped God, saying:
"Amen! Blessing and glory and wisdom,
Thanksgiving and honor and power and might,
Be to our God forever and ever. Amen."

Photo by Linda

Pachystachys lutea, known by the common names Lollipop Plant and Golden Shrimp Plant, is a subtropical, soft-stemmed evergreen shrub between 36 and 48 inches tall. The long-throated, short-lived white flowers emerge sequentially from overlapping bright yellow bracts on racemes that are produced throughout the warm months. It is a popular landscape plant in tropical and subtropical areas of the world. They grow in almost any well-drained soil but, like most ornamentals, prefer a soil with an acid reaction. In this preferred medium they attain their maximum in leaf size and beautiful coloring. (From Wikipedia).

Life Application:

The Lollipop plant shows forth praise, glory, and honor to the King of Kings, our Savior, Jesus. All that we are, or ever hope to be, is linked to our daily fellowship and commune with our Creator.

Spend time today walking and talking with Jesus. Praise Him first. Then, have a conversation with Him, such as "What is on your agenda for me today? What is your direction and plan? How can I encourage or minister to others?" Tell Him your joys—laugh with Him. Tell Him your sorrows or disappointments; but do not linger there.

Stop! Look! Listen! Observe the beauty of the earth—the skies, trees, flowers. As you release your hopes, doubts, disappointments, and fears to Jesus, He will listen, comfort, calm you, and give you peace and direction.

If you are having difficulty hearing Jesus, perhaps you are too myopic about the cares of your life and are worrying more than you are praying and praising.

Slow down! Put electronic devices aside! Get in the scriptures—NOT Leviticus or Numbers! Listen to your best friend—Jesus! Honor, serve, and prefer others today, in Jesus' name!

Blessings, and praise God from whom all blessings flow!

No Worry

Alstroemeria – Peruvian Lily

Matthew 6:28-30

28 So why do you worry about clothing? Consider the lilies of the field, how they grow: they neither toil nor spin; 29 and yet I say to you that even Solomon in all his glory was not arrayed like one of these. 30 Now if God so clothes the grass of the field, which today is, and tomorrow is thrown into the oven, will He not much more clothe you, O you of little faith?

Psalm 34:5

They looked to Him and were radiant, and their faces were not ashamed.

Photo by Linda

Alstroemeria, commonly called the Peruvian lily or Lily of the Incas, is a genus of flowering plants in the family Alstroemeriaceae. They are all native to South America although some have become naturalized in the United States, Mexico, Australia, New Zealand, Madeira and the Canary Islands.

Plants of this genus grow from a cluster of tubers. They send up fertile and sterile stems, the fertile stems of some species reaching 1.5 meters in height. The leaves are variable in shape and the blades have smooth edges. The flowers are solitary or borne in short stalks that spread out from one point (umbels). The flower has six petals (outer part of the flower) each up to 5 centimeters long. They come in many shades of red, orange, purple, green, and white, flecked and striped and streaked with darker colors. (Wikipedia)

Life Application:

Two years ago, we had this beauty. Last year, I ordered one by mail, but it was small and did not bloom. If you see this plant at a nursery, please let me know. I could not find one this year. It is easy to grow. It is used widely in cut arrangements {weddings, funerals, and other arrangements}, and the flowers last several days; but, just do not over-water.

In the midst of a great Satanic attack on our country, Satan is on a rampage. Millions of Christians (world-wide) are praying. We must not give in to the thugs who steal, kill, and destroy—Satanic influence through anti-Christ, anarchist, and ungodly billionaires.

Our hope is in Jesus! We must war in prayer! Our country is moving toward socialism, anarchy, Marxism, and the destruction of our Christian heritage and the Constitution. However, revival is coming! Pray! Pray! Pray!

Stand up for Jesus and "consider the lilies of the field, how they grow; they neither toil nor spin." As we look to Jesus—the Author and Finisher of our faith—we are "radiant," and our faces are "not ashamed."

Blessings, and praise God from whom all blessings flow!

Angel Wing

Begonia

2 Corinthians 11:13-14

For such are false apostles, deceitful workers, transforming themselves into apostles of Christ. And no wonder! For Satan himself transforms himself into an angel of light.

Photo by Linda

Angel Wing begonia plants, first found in South America, make up a large portion of the cane begonia group. Angel wing begonias have large, "angel wing" shaped, dark green leaves, often with metallic silver specks. The underside of the plant leaf is usually a deep red. Angel wing begonias produce hanging clusters of delicate flowers in red, white, orange, or pink. The intensity of the color of the flowers and leaves depends upon how much light the plant gets. Angel wing begonias are beautiful, easy- care, flowering plants that brighten your home all year. They are considered poisonous and should be kept away from pets and children (Wikipedia).

Our beautiful Angel Wing Begonias are in hanging baskets and enjoy mostly shade, with partial sun. They need daily watering when outside. They are easy care and have beautiful red or pink flower clusters. This year, we have a red, a yellow, a pink, and peach plants. They are beautiful!!!

George Soros is a Hungarian-Jewish-American left-wing socialist, anarchist, billionaire, and "a well-known supporter of progressive and liberal political causes to which he dispenses donations through his foundation—the Open Society Foundations." Soros is known as "The Man Who Broke the Bank of England" as a result of his short sale of $10 billion worth of pounds sterling, which made him a profit of $1 billion, during the 1992 Black Wednesday UK currency crisis (Wikipedia). The Open Society Foundation sometimes hires people to go across state lines and on college campuses to riot and pillage, to protest conservative values and speakers, and to destroy public property. He is considered by God, an "angel of light," a messenger of Satan, an ANTI-CHRIST. Outwardly his programs may look beautiful, but those programs are poisonous, anti-American, and anti-Christ. Pray for his exposure and downfall in Jesus' name!

Revelation 12:11

And they overcame him by the blood of the Lamb and by the word of their testimony, and they did not love their lives to the death.

Blessings, and praise God from whom all blessings flow!

Know Your Place In Christ

Lantana

Psalm 20:6-8 NLT

*6 Now I know that the Lord rescues his anointed king.
He will answer him from his holy heaven
and rescue him by his great power.
7 Some nations boast of their chariots and horses,
but we boast in the name of the Lord our God.
8 Those nations will fall down and collapse,
but we will rise up and stand firm.*

Photo by Linda

The lantanas are very free flowering from spring until frost. The new varieties are dwarf, spreading and bushy, early blooming and free-flowering, and are available in a much wider color range—from white through yellow, orange, to deep red, hot pink and purple. Often the older outer flowers of each cluster are of a different hue than the younger, inner ones. The Spanish colonists used lantanas medicinally to make infusions to be taken as medicine and used in baths; and in Sinaloa, the plant is a favorite remedy for snake bites—a poultice of crushed leaves is applied to the wound (Wikipedia) (I know—too much information).

The lantana reminds me of the Christian who knows who he/she is in Christ—bold, strong, courageous, and daring, He knows of and has experienced the rescuing power of God.

Some may trust in military, economic, and financial strength; nevertheless, in uncertain times "we boast in the name of the Lord our God."

Our country in the past, presently, and in the future has and will experience the horrors and fears of wars, floods, famine, earthquakes, financial despair, internal combustion, and economic uncertainty. It is extremely important to stand for God's purposes and to be involved in our country. Some leaders call right wrong and wrong right; however, we must not lose focus! We must stand firmly on God's word.

Those people or nations who deny our God "will fall down and collapse, but we will rise up and stand firm." Be an example of Jesus to those around you—"rescue the perishing, care for the dying." Love, honor, serve, and prefer others.

Blessings, and praise God from whom all blessings flow!

Redeemed

Variegated Jew

Revelation 5:9-10

And they sang a new song, saying:
"You are worthy to take the scroll, And to open its seals;
For You were slain,
And have redeemed us to God by Your blood
Out of every tribe and tongue and people and nation,
And have made us kings and priests to our God;
And we shall reign on the earth."

Photo by Linda

Tradescantia pallida is an evergreen perennial plant of scrambling stature. It is distinguished by elongated, pointed leaves - themselves glaucous green, fringed with red or purple—and bearing small, sterile three-petaled flowers of white, pink or purple. Plants are top-killed by moderate frosts, but will often sprout back from roots (Wikipedia).

We have two different types of Jew plant—purple and variegated. The variegated plant reminds me of the stripes on Jesus' back. We did have a beautiful red Jew, but it is difficult to find. If the Jew plants are in the ground, they will die down, but come back in the spring. If they are in an outside pot, they will die.

"For as in Adam all die, even so in Christ all shall be made alive." (1 Corinthians 12: 22) The above verses remind me of Jesus' royal redemption for us— "every tribe and people and nation."

"He paid a debt He did not owe.
I owed a debt I could not pay.
I needed someone to wash my sins away."

Anonymous

Blessings, and praise God from whom all blessings flow!

Endurance

Wave Petunias

James 1:12 NLT

God blesses those who patiently endure testing and temptation. Afterward they will receive the crown of life that God has promised to those who love him.

Photo by Linda

The wave petunias are very low-maintenance and can withstand extremes of heat and cold, rain and humidity. The wave flowers bloom lavishly well into fall and sometimes completely through the winter in warmer areas of Texas (Wikipedia).

I have not had great success with the old variety of petunias. Although they are beautiful, when the heat comes in late May and June, those varieties get burned by the heat. The wave petunias remind me of the above verse. They endure the testing of extreme heat. Have a selah (pause and think) moment.

How can I endure testing and temptation? Consider and meditate on the following statement.

Although I pray, consume the scriptures, praise and worship the Lord, I am privileged to walk and talk with a godly brother, Bob Denton. We rarely see each other; nevertheless, we have been spiritual accountability partners for 40 years plus—through storms, losses, joys, and blessings. Accountability is essential to the Christian walk!

Blessings, and praise God from whom all blessings flow!

Majestic Beauty

Pride of Barbados

Revelation 19:16

And He has on His robe and on His thigh a name written:
"KING OF KINGS AND
LORD OF LORDS."

Photo by Linda

The Pride of Barbados is an unusual plant. The blooms have incredible flower clusters showing an orange-red with a tinge of gold on the edges. Each flower is composed of five showy petals with very prominent six inch long red stamens. This makes the Pride of Barbados one of the most attractive heat loving plants for San Antonio. The plant grows fairly fast and can be up to 12 feet tall and spread 10 feet wide. The top is round in shape with wide spreading branches. The stems and branches also have sharp thorns or spines (Wikipedia).

In our area this beauty will die back during the winter and come back in the spring.

1 Chronicles 16:29

Give to the Lord the glory due His name;
Bring an offering, and come before Him.
O, worship the Lord in the beauty of holiness!

Blessings, and praise God from whom all blessings flow!

Earthkind Roses

Proverbs 16:3

*Commit your works to the LORD,
And your thoughts will be established.*

Proverbs 3:5-6

*Trust in the LORD with all your heart,
And lean not on your own understanding;
6 In all your ways acknowledge Him,
And He shall direct your paths.*

Photo by Linda

Earth Kind is a special designation awarded only to those roses demonstrating superior pest tolerance, combined with outstanding landscape performance. Earth Kind roses do well in a variety of soil types, ranging from well-drained acidic sands to poorly aerated, highly alkaline clays. Once established, these select cultivars also have excellent heat and drought tolerance, while limiting the use of fertilizers, pesticides, and water (Wikipedia).

Our 21 rose plants will bloom through the time of intense heat, and they will not die. As we commit our ways to the Lord, we will be established so that we will weather the heat (trials); and we will be sustained to fulfill His purpose. We can only see where we have been! God knows the future, and the plans He has for us!

We have several "Hybrid Tea Roses" that are extremely beautiful; however, if there is too much moisture on their leaves, they are prone to the fungus—"black spot." I use a fungicide spray that controls well, even though I lost a plant yesterday to the fungus.

"Black spot" fungus represents our sins. This fungus starts with a black spot on the leaves. Then, the leaves turn yellow and drop off the stem. If not treated, the stem begins to blacken and die. Just as black spot can kill the rose bush, sin can destroy us and make us callus to our actions. It can destroy us spiritually, which separates us from our relationship with God.

Please do not "frustrate" the grace of God in your life and make unwise and ungodly decisions that would lead you out of the will of God for a season of pleasure—greed, sexual sins, or the "pride of life." The time of extreme heat, storms, wanderings, and trials is for a season. If one turns to Christ, there is forgiveness and redemption. If one does not turn to Christ, there is turmoil and consequences. Consequences of sin are journey changing, yet they are redeemable through Christ!

Stay focused on God! Be steadfast and unmovable in the scriptures and prayer to KNOW God! You will bloom again!

Results:

1. Commit yourself to the Lord and you will be established!
2. Trust in the Lord completely!
3. Ask God to remove your pride! Do not rely on your own "stinking"' thinking!
4. Acknowledge God—give Him the credit for your success!
5. Then, God will guide your direction in life's journey!

Blessings, and praise God from whom all blessings flow!

Purity through Redemption

Amaryllis

Song of Solomon 2:1

I am the rose of Sharon, And the lily of the valleys.

Photo by Linda

Of all flowering bulbs, amaryllis are the easiest to bring to bloom. This can be accomplished indoors or out, and over an extended period of time. The amaryllis originated in South America's tropical regions. It's botanical name is Hippeastrum. The large flowers and ease with which they can be brought to bloom make amaryllis popular and in demand worldwide. The amaryllis comes in many beautiful varieties including various shades of red, white, pink, salmon and orange (Wikipedia).

We have two plants—one white and one red. The white plant reminds me of the purity of Jesus. "For you know that God paid a ransom to save you from the empty life you inherited from your ancestors. And it was not paid with mere gold or silver, which lose their value. It was the precious blood of Christ, the sinless, spotless Lamb of God" (1 Peter 1:18-19 NLT).

The red plant reminds me of redemption. "And they sang a new song, saying: 'You are worthy to take the scroll, and to open its seals; for You were slain, and have redeemed us to God by Your blood out of every tribe and tongue and people and nation,'" (Revelation 5:9).

Blessings, and praise God from whom all blessings flow!

Time in the Word

Daisies

Isaiah 40:8

The grass withers, the flower fades, but the word of our God stands forever.

Photo by Linda

Daisies are distinguished by a flower composed of 15 to 30 white ray flowers surrounding a bright yellow disk flower. The oxeye daisy is native to Europe and Asia, and it has become a common wild plant in the United States. This perennial grows to a height of about 2 feet and has oblong, incised leaves and long petioles (leafstalks). Its solitary flowers are about 1 to 2 inches in diameter, and the ray flowers are white in color. (Britannica).

We have 60 or 70 Shasta daisies. I have also seen them growing wild on farmland. These proud, erect beauties remind me of the above verse. God's Word is powerful and necessary for our daily existence. God's Word IS our daily spiritual bread (Matthew 6:11); a cleansing agent (Psalm 119:9); Wonderful Counselor (Isaiah 9:6); the Way, the Truth and the Life (Purpose) (John 14:6); a Lamp and Light (Psalm 119:105); the Alpha and Omega (Totality) (Revelation 1:8) and several hundred other things too numerous to list at this time.

Read the Word! Meditate on the Word! Sing the Word! Pray the Word! Any other answer outside of God's Word is NOT true ("sinking sand") and will not be blessed by God!

Blessings, and praise God from whom all blessings flow!

Boug ainvillea

Psalm 96:6-9 NKJ

6 *Honor and majesty are before Him;*
Strength and beauty are in His sanctuary.
7 *Give to the LORD, O families of the peoples,*
Give to the LORD glory and strength.
8 *Give to the LORD the glory due His name;*
Bring an offering, and come into His courts.
9 *Oh, worship the LORD in the beauty of holiness!*
Tremble before Him, all the earth.

Photo by Linda

Our Bougainvilleas are an iridescent pink and one magenta. The actual flower of the plant is small and generally white, but each cluster of three flowers is surrounded by three or six bracts with the bright colored leaves associated with the plant, including pink, magenta, purple, red, orange, white, or yellow. This plant is beautifully strange in that the small, white, delicate, and dainty flower protrudes out of a colored leaf. The Bougainvillea has thorns and a toxic sap which (if you are pricked) can produce a skin rash (Wikipedia).

When you view this plant, you are overwhelmed by the beauty of the leaves, not so much by the gorgeous, small, white flower. It is like the brightly colored leaves are drawing attention to the beauty of the flower God has given them.

Life Application:

Regardless of our station in life, even the most spiritually outwardly beautiful or, spiritually outwardly ugly can be used as gold in our Master Jesus' hands. (Remember, the Lord looks inwardly. We look outwardly). As we yield our total being to Christ, He can remove the toxicity of our hurts which can cause betrayal, jealousy, doubt, greed, lying, cheating, adultery, arrogant pride, unbelief, and discord among believers, slander, lack of love, lack of loyalty, and lack of knowing how to honor, serve, and prefer others.

Nevertheless, when we realize how needy, how lacking, and rebellious we are, and repent before Jesus—give up our self-imposed rights—we run to Jesus to let him speak to us, train us, and mold us as clay in HIS hand. After true humility, confession of sins, and repentance (change our mind set) from our old ways—THEN, Jesus offers love, joy, peace, and acceptance, and He guides and empowers us by the Holy Spirit. He removes the toxicity and trains us into His life's purpose and plan for our lives.

Blessings, and praise God from whom all blessings flow!

Choose Joy

Ruellia – Mexican Petunia

Psalm 16:11 NLT

You will show me the way of life,
granting me the joy of your presence
and the pleasures of living with you forever.

Psalm 37:4 NLT

Take delight in the Lord, and he will give you your heart's desires.

Photo by Linda

The Mexican petunia, Ruellia, or Wild petunia, is a three-foot-tall evergreen shrub and bears many tubular blue or purple, petunia-like flowers on dark stems over a long period. Each flower lasts for just one day. It is a fast grower that may self-seed aggressively.

It blooms from spring to frost, is native to Mexico and the southwestern U.S. and has no serious problems (Wikipedia).

I love this plant!!! It is beautanimous! (Warning: This plant is very invasive.)

Linda and I shared with our kids, and I also shared with my students at times that happiness is a choice of the mind. Due to unpleasant circumstances, I can be happy or sad, feel sorry for myself or pour myself into other people. Take time today, regardless of the circumstances, to sing to the Lord—your own made-up song. Thank Him for your many blessings. Thank Him and pray for the people around you—acquaintances, friends, co-workers, those in authority over you, and even those you do not like.

Life is too short for us to be myopic. The Lord has gifted each of us in so many ways. The Ruellia flower lasts just one day, but it will flower again the next day. "The steadfast love of the Lord NEVER changes. His mercies NEVER come to an end. They are new every morning." (Lamentations 3:22-23 KJV) Great is His faithfulness to us!

Encourage, love, honor, serve, and prefer others today!

Blessings, and praise God from whom all blessings flow!

Celosia

Cock's Comb

Psalm 40: 16

Let all those who seek You rejoice and be glad in You;
Let such as love Your salvation say continually, The Lord be magnified!

Philippians 4:4

Rejoice in the Lord always. Again I will say, rejoice!

Photo by Linda

Cockscombs (Celosia) are a small genus of edible and ornamental plants in the amaranth family, Amaranthaceae. The generic name is derived from the Greek word (kelos), meaning "burned," and refers to the flame-like flower heads. Species are commonly known as woolflowers, or, if the flower heads are crested by fasciation, cockscombs. Celosia is known as a foodstuff in Indonesia and India. Seed production in these species can be very high, 200–700 kg per hectare. Depending upon the location and fertility of the soil, blossoms can last 8–10 weeks. This beautiful annual plant can grow to a height of 24–36 inches. It enjoys full sun, poses no danger, has bright colors—red, orange, bright yellow, white/near white, and blue-green foliage. It blooms from mid-summer to mid-fall (Plant Files).

Life Application:

One can realize only minutely what a wonderful imagination and color scheme our God has given to us. We (as the celosia) come in all manners of colors, shapes, and sizes. God has created us to love, honor, rejoice, and glorify Him and to tell others about His great redemptive, grace, and mercy.

1 John 3:1

Behold what manner of love the Father has bestowed on us,
that we should be called children of God!

Romans 5:8

But God demonstrates His own love toward us,
in that while we were still sinners, Christ died for us.

Blessings, and praise God from whom all blessings flow!

Chinese Fringe

Psalm 116:1-2

1 I love the LORD, because He has heard
My voice and my supplications.
2 Because He has inclined His ear to me,
Therefore I will call upon Him as long as I live.

Chinese Fringe Flower is a species native to eastern Asia, in eastern and central China, Korea, and Japan. It is cultivated in Europe and North America as an ornamental tree, valued for its feathery red flower heads. It is a deciduous shrub or small to medium-sized tree. Wikipedia).

Our plant really struggled a few years ago in a large pot. The beautiful feathery flowers reminded me of how fragile our lives are. I removed it from the pot and planted it in the garden soil. I pruned, watered, prayed, and fertilized; hence it made a wonderful recovery and was six feet tall before the freeze of February 2021.

It is so necessary for us to discover what really is important in our daily lives. We plan, work, provide for our families, grow old, become frozen and overheated by life's storms, and die. Is that all there is??? NO!!! NO!!! NO!!!

We are empowered by our God and His plan for our lives. (Jer 29:11) He hears our voice and collects our tears. (Ps 56:8) He rejoices over us with singing. (Zephaniah 3:17) He walks with us through the storms. (Is 41:10; 43:1-3) He prunes, waters, fertilizes us by His presence and His word and gives us direction, peace beyond understanding, and most importantly—His LOVE.

"Therefore, I will call upon Him as long as I live" (Ps 116:2) (Please read the above scripture references)!

Blessings, and praise God from whom all blessings flow!

God Cares

Vinca – Periwinkle

Psalm 149:3

Let them praise His name with the dance;
Let them sing praises to Him with the timbrel and harp.

Nehemiah 8:10

For this day is holy to our Lord. Do not sorrow,
for the joy of the Lord is your strength.

Photo by Linda

Abundant blooms and ease of care make vinca (Catharanthus roseus) an excellent selection if you have little time to tend your garden. Useful in borders, flowerbeds, rock gardens and containers, the vinca flower provides instant color wherever it grows. The round, flat blooms appear on top of 12 to 15-inch stems. These drought-tolerant bedding plants thrive in any soil type as long as it is fast draining and not overly fertile (Wikipedia).

The Periwinkle is such a joyous and happy plant. It smiles at us. I am reminded of the above verses.

During good times and bad our Lord loves us, smiles upon us, and cares deeply for us. America reminds me of many Old Testament stories of how Israel forsook God, and they made and worshipped idols. Yet, God with His everlasting love and mercy always provided a way of forgiveness and rescue. There is no true joy or happiness without our relationship with Jesus!

2 Chronicles 7:14

If My people who are called by My name will humble themselves, and pray and seek My face, and turn from their wicked ways, then I will hear from heaven, and will forgive their sin and heal their land.

Blessings, and praise God from whom all blessings flow!

Stand on God's Word

Marigold

Isaiah 60:1

Arise, shine; For your light has come!
And the glory of the Lord is risen upon you.

Photo by Linda

Native to South America, Mexico and the southwestern United States, marigolds (Tagetes spp.) have been found in gardens worldwide for hundreds of years. Because of their cheerful bright orange and yellow blooms, ease of care and few problems with insects and disease, marigolds continue to be a popular bedding plant in the United States. Some gardeners also plant marigolds in vegetable gardens because they believe the flower can protect plants from insect pests, although research studies have not supported these claims (Wikipedia).

Isaiah 60:1

Arise, shine; For your light has come!
And the glory of the Lord is risen upon you.

We love our marigold plants. They are bright, cheerful, and radiant and remind me of the above verse. I am totally amazed, yet not surprised how deficient so many Christians are in the scriptures. If we are Christians, we should be reading the scriptures daily for comfort, guidance, direction, and WISDOM.

I know that the readers of these devotional series read the scriptures daily; however, there are many seniors who are content to listen and believe fake news, rather than research the truth. They are paralyzed by partial truths and lies rather than going to God's scriptures.

I have two elderly relatives who are content to die rather than take the time to stand on the scriptural promises and to see what God's agenda is. That's a Shame! Rise up O men and women of God!

Read God's word! Meditate on God's word! Believe God's word! Pray God's word! Sing God's word!

Blessings, and praise God from whom all blessings flow!

Sorrow Replaced by Joy

Crape Myrtles

Isaiah 51:11

Those who have been ransomed (redeemed) by the Lord will return.
They will enter Jerusalem singing,
crowned with everlasting joy.
Sorrow and mourning will disappear,
and they will be filled with joy and gladness.

Photo by Linda

I love our 22 Crape myrtles. Two species make up most of our cultivated flowering types, but there are 5 species and approximately 120 varieties listed on the McKinney Trails web site. Several are tropical timber trees.

The Crape myrtle was introduced to the United States over 200 years ago from Southeast Asia and Japan. (McKinney Trails) (Wikipedia).

Our garden has eight different shades of colors. These plants are drought resistant, mostly disease resistant, mostly pest resistant (not unto death), proud, joyful, sturdy, and glad singers to our Lord, God Almighty.

As we realize who we are in Jesus—ransomed and redeemed—bought and paid for by the blood of Jesus Christ, we become energized as we praise and worship our King of Kings. We are driven by the fact that we may know God (not just about God) as we consume His Word. "Sorrow and mourning will disappear, and we will be filled with joy and gladness."

Love, honor, serve, and prefer others today. Forgive one another. Be a representative of Jesus!

Blessings, and praise God from whom all blessings flow!

Jesus, Our Rose of Sharon

Song of Solomon 2:1

I am the rose of Sharon, and the lily of the valleys.

Photo by Linda

Althaea is a genus of herbaceous perennial plants native to Europe, North Africa and western Asia. It includes Althaea officinalis, also known as the marshmallow plant, whence the fluffy confection got its name. They are found on the banks of rivers and in salt marshes, preferring moist, sandy soils. The stems grow to 1–2 m (39 inches to 6. 5 feet) tall, and flower in mid-summer. The leaves are palmately lobed with 3–7 lobes.

Althaea species are used as food plants. The traditional medicinal uses of the plant are reflected in the name of the genus, which comes from the Greek althainein, meaning "to heal." The flowers and young leaves can be eaten, and are often added to salads or are boiled and fried. The roots and stem also secrete mucilage, which is used to soften the skin. It is used in cosmetic treatments.

The Rose of Sharon (Hibiscus syriacus) also known as an Althea shrub is a mid-summer bloomer in white, pink, red, or purple with a red center. You can also find them ruffled in the same array of colors including what many call blue (Wikipedia).

We added this beautiful flower to our garden two years ago. I will probably make a small tree out of it. This plant reminds me of the characteristics of Jesus:

Galatians 5:22-23

But the fruit of the Spirit is love, joy, peace, longsuffering, kindness, goodness, faithfulness, gentleness, self-control.

Blessings, and praise God from whom all blessings flow!

Great Is Your Faithfulness

Hydrangea

Lamentations 3:22-23

Through the Lord's mercies we are not consumed, because His compassions fail not. They are new every morning; Great is Your faithfulness.

Photos by Linda

With dozens of species and even more varieties, hydrangeas (Hydrangea spp.) have been popular garden plants for decades. Their flowers now come in a wide array of colors, including bright blue, deep red, and pale green. Some hydrangeas have large, round flower clusters while others have smaller, flatter more delicate flowers. The foliage also varies depending on the species.

These versatile shrubs thrive in sandy coastal soils, shady woodland sites, and almost everything in between. To ensure that hydrangea shrubs have time to establish a healthy root system before blooming, it is best to plant them in fall or early spring.

Once planted, hydrangeas are rapid growers, averaging 2 feet or more of growth per year and may grow upwards to 15 feet tall. Hydrangeas are toxic to people and animals (Wikipedia).

The Hydrangea bush to me is a symbol of the Lord's peace, steadfast love and mercy, and faithfulness.

"The steadfast love of the Lord never ceases.
His mercies they never come to an end.
They are new every morning.
They are new every morning.
Great is Thy faithfulness O Lord."

McNeill

Blessings, and praise God from whom all blessings flow!

Rudbeckia

Isaiah 60:1

Arise, shine; for your light has come!
And the glory of the Lord is risen upon you.

Photo by Linda

Rudbeckias are perennial flowering plants that are hardy in Zones 4–9. Like many plants, they have several common names, among which are: Black-eyed Susan, Gloriosa Daisy, and Yellow Ox Eye. They are members of the Asteraceae family and are native to both damp woodlands and dry prairies in North America (Wikipedia).

It has been several years since I planted this beautiful, sunshine plant; consequently, when I saw this at the nursery I had to have it. I remember singing the above verse in the 1980s and 1990s.

Rudbeckia reminds me of the majesty and glory of Jesus. When I was 13 years old, my grandmother was on her death bed at her home. She had been in so much pain; however, all of a sudden, her face brightened, and she smiled. She spoke to her previously departed sister, and then, she said, "The flowers are so beautiful! The colors are so bright and glorious! The music is so wonderful!" Then, she died and went to be with Jesus!!!

"Majesty, worship his majesty!
Unto Jesus be all glory, honor, and praise!
Majesty, kingdom authority flow from his throne,
unto his own, his anthem raise.
So exalt, lift up on high the name of Jesus!
Magnify, come glorify Christ Jesus, the King!
Majesty, worship his majesty!
Jesus who died, now glorified, King of all kings!
So exalt, lift up on high the name of Jesus!
Magnify, come glorify Christ Jesus, the King!
Majesty, worship his majesty!
Jesus who died, now glorified, King of all kings!
Jesus who died, now glorified, King of all kings!"

Songwriter: Jack Hayford

Blessings, and praise God from whom all blessings flow!

God's Humorous Creativity

Chenille Plant

Psalm 148:1

Praise the Lord!
Praise the Lord from the heavens;
Praise Him in the heights!

Photo by Linda

The chenlille plant (Acalypha hispida), a member of the spurge family, is named for the French word for caterpillar. Its crimson accents can provide textural interest to a sunny flower garden or a homegrown bouquet. The foliage of the chenille plant is unremarkable; the real stars are its fuzzy red flowers (Wikipedia).

This unusual flower shows the tremendous imagination and creative power of our God. It is just fun!

"All Things Bright & Beautiful
All creatures great and small,
All things wise and wonderful,
The Lord God made them all.

"Each little flower that opens,
Each little bird that sings,
He made their glowing colours,
He made their tiny wings."
Composed by John Rutter

Blessings, and praise God from whom all blessings flow!

Loud Praise to God!

Crossandra

Psalm 145:1-3

I will extol You, my God, O King; and, I will bless Your name forever and ever. Every day I will bless You, and I will praise Your name forever and ever. Great is the Lord, and greatly to be praised; and His greatness is unsearchable.

Photo by Linda

Crossandra is a genus of plants in the family Acanthaceae, comprising 54 species that occur in Indonesia, Malaysia, Africa, Brazil, Central America, Madagascar, Arabia and the Indian subcontinent. Some species, especially

Crossandra infundibuliformis, are cultivated for their brightly colored flowers. Representatives of the family can be found in nearly every habitat, including dense or open forests, scrublands, wet fields and valleys, sea coast and marine areas, swamps, and mangrove forests (Wikipedia).

Two years ago, we bought this colorful, orange plant. I could not find one last year, but this year, I found and bought one. This plant will awaken you!

Psalm 150:5

Praise Him with loud cymbals; Praise Him with clashing cymbals!

Who can praise our God enough?

Blessings, and praise God from whom all blessings flow!

Shine in a Dark World

Buttercup

Psalm 34:5

They looked to Him and were radiant, and their faces were not ashamed.

Ranunculus spp., or buttercup, is a family of bright and attractive flowers that can be found in shades of yellow, red, orange, pink, white, and lavender. Perhaps one of the significant reasons it got its name buttercup, aside from the fact that it does look like a cup filled with butter, is the ancient folklore common in the southern regions. It was told that if you hold the ranunculus flower under your chin and it turns yellow, it means you like butter (Vigra World).

Two years ago was the first time that we grew this flower. It reminds me of the following verse.

2 Corinthians 4:6

For it is the God who commanded light to shine out of darkness,
who has shone in our hearts to give the light of the knowledge
of the glory of God in the face of Jesus Christ.

Blessings, and praise God from whom all blessings flow!

Airplane or Spider Plant

Psalm 96:6

Honor and majesty are before Him; Strength and beauty are in His sanctuary.

Photo by Linda

The graceful, easy care indoor spider (or airplane) plant, that can also grow outdoors in the shade during the summer, produces leaves directly from the center of the plant. When kept root-bound, an airplane plant sends out numerous long stems with baby plants at the ends that can easily be used for propagation.

Spider plants or Airplane plants, Chlorophytum comosumare, are available with green leaves, green leaves trimmed in white, or white leaves trimmed in green. All varieties are easy to care for and fun to have. (House Plant 411.com)

My mother grew this strange wonder. We have had this beauty for several years, and I have rooted additional plants. I know the above verse may seem strange for this plant; however, when you really behold and realize that each small segment or baby plant can be cut off and rooted immediately in dirt to grow a new plant, you must know the magnificence and wonder of God's creative power to create all things—especially us! O, how He loves you and me!

Blessings, and praise God from whom all blessings flow!

Blue Daze Inspires Joy

Psalm 105:43

He brought out His people with joy, His chosen ones with gladness.

Photo by Linda

A native of Brazil and Paraguay, blue daze is a suitable landscape plant for USDA zones 8 to 11. It prefers full sunlight, though it will welcome some afternoon shade. Flowering may be reduced in areas that are too shady. Blue daze is tolerant of salty conditions, including direct salt spray, making it an excellent choice for coastal gardens. It does well in containers and can be cultivated in a pot or hanging basket (Wikipedia).

This plant is a beautiful vibrant blue, and it reminds me of the joy, happiness, and gladness which are demonstrated in our lives as we daily read, meditate, pray, sing, and believe God's word.

> "I will sing new songs of gladness.
> I will sing Jehovah's praises upon a ten-stringed psaltery.
> Every day will I extol Thee and will bless Thy holy name.
> I will bless Thy holy name.
> Great is God and great His mercy; who shall tell of all His greatness?
> Who shall His power declare?"
> Biblical Songs by Antonin Dvorak

Blessings, and praise God from whom all blessings flow!

Hallelujah!

Silver Falls

Revelation 19:6

And I heard, as it were, the voice of a great multitude, as the sound of many waters and as the sound of mighty thunderings, saying, "Halleluiah! For the Lord God Omnipotent reigns!"

Photo by Linda

"Bless the Lord, O my soul! Praise the Lord" (Ps 104: 35)! Praise the Lord is the definition of "Hallelujah" It is used in many psalms and in the book of Revelation (Vine's Complete Expository Dictionary of Old and New Testament Words).

Dichondra argentea 'Silver Falls' is a creeping, trailing herbaceous perennial that is native to the desert regions of the United States and Mexico. It makes a great bedding plant and its silvery foliage contrasts well with other green-leaved plants. This plant can grow in sandy loam soil and is best suited for containers, hanging baskets, rock walls, as a ground cover, window boxes, or an accent plant in beds. This plant does not have major insect, pest, or disease problems.(Wikipedia).

We enjoy this plant. This year I reversed the planting, and I put the Silver Falls above the Blue Daze plant. I like the way this plant drapes. It reminds me of the "Waterfall Hallelujah" song of the 1980s and Handel's "Hallelujah Chorus."

"King of Kings and Lord of Lords, King of Kings and Lord of Lords
And he shall reign forever and ever (And he shall reign forever and ever)
Forever and ever, forever and ever (King of Kings and Lord of Lords)
Hallelujah! Hallelujah! Hallelujah! Hallelujah! Hallelujah!"
A portion of the Hallelujah Chorus by G.F. Handel

Blessings, and praise God from whom all blessings flow!

Petchoa Supercal

Ecclesiastes 3:11

He has made everything beautiful in its time.
Also, He has put eternity in their hearts, except that
no one can find out the work that God does from beginning to end.

Photo by Linda

The Petchoa Supercal is a super hybrid with large vibrant flowers. It has continuous blooms from spring into fall until the first hard frost and has exceptional garden performance in spite of late spring frosts, rain or summer heat. It is superb for containers and hanging baskets and loved by hummingbirds. Petchoa is a hybrid between petunias and calibrachoas (Wikipedia).

This plant is gorgeous, and I could not resist buying these different colors last year. Even the Godliest and the vilest of humanity have a longing in their hearts for the eternal God.

Isaiah 57:15

For thus says the High and Lofty One who inhabits eternity, whose name is Holy: "I dwell in the high and holy place, with him who has a contrite and humble spirit, to revive the spirit of the humble, and to revive the heart of the contrite ones."

Blessings, and praise God from whom all blessings flow!

Patience

Impatiens

Galatians 5:22-23 AMP

But the fruit of the Spirit [the result of His presence within us] is love [unselfish concern for others], joy, [inner] peace, patience [not the ability to wait, but how we act while waiting], kindness, goodness, faithfulness, gentleness, self-control. Against such things there is no law.

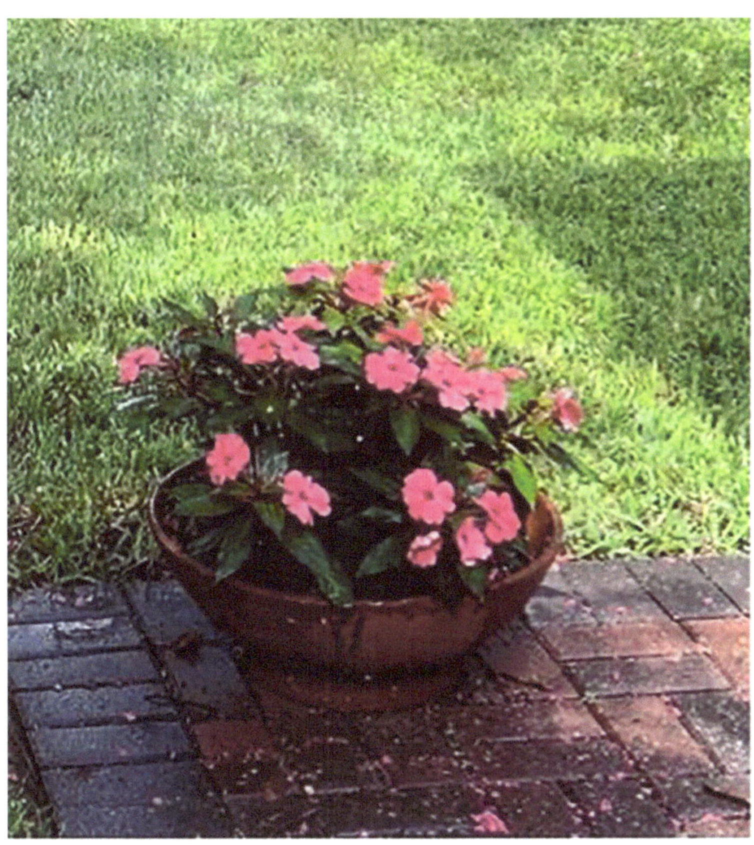

Photo by Linda

Impatiens is a beautiful annual that makes an excellent houseplant or summer bedding and container plant. Impatiens is also known as "Busy Lizzie," and its name is a Latin word that describes the way its seeds shoot out of its pods when ripe (the slightest touch can make a ripe impatiens seed pod burst open and scatter its seeds). Generally, impatiens like shade and moisture (Wikipedia).

I have practiced the art of trying to be patient for many years. At times, I have succeeded—but sometimes not. I once told my sons that "I think that I am the most patient person in the world." Our oldest son, Asa III said—"Well, dad, you don't know many people, do you?" Out of the mouths of family, there is truth.

However, those of us who have been pursuing the Lord for a long time desire all of the fruit of the Spirit so that we may know God and be obedient to Him.

James 1: 2-4

My brethren, count it all joy when you fall into various trials, 3 knowing that the testing of your faith produces patience. But let patience have its perfect work, that you may be perfect (mature) and complete, lacking nothing.

Blessings, and praise God from whom all blessings flow!

Wishbone Flower

Ezekiel 17: 8

It was planted in good soil by many waters, to bring forth branches, bear fruit, and become a majestic vine.

Photo by Linda

Wishbone flowers (Torenia fournieri) are an excellent choice for bringing some color and life to a shadier part of the garden. Unlike many other flowers, these compact plants don't mind growing in a little shade. Their trumpet-shaped blooms come in several color choices; the primary species coloring is a dark blue-purple and lavender with yellow markings. Within each flower, a pair of stamens (the slender stalks) unite in a shape that resembles a wishbone, hence the plant's common name. While they are annuals and will die once frost arrives, they grow quickly and bloom profusely from early summer all the way until cold weather sets in. Moreover, the plants are deer-resistant and attractive to hummingbirds (Wikipedia).

This flower is joyful! Three years ago, this plant was struggling; therefore, I moved it and reduced the amount of sun it was getting; and now, it is thriving.

Psalm 139:15

My frame was not hidden from You, when I was made in secret,
and skillfully wrought in the lowest parts of the earth.

The Lord knows our sensitivities, our hopes, and our desires.

Psalm 139:14

I will praise You, for I am fearfully and wonderfully made;
marvelous are Your works, and that my soul knows very well.

Blessings, and praise God from whom all blessings flow!

Vitex (Texas Lilac)

Song of Solomon 1:3

Because of the fragrance of your good ointments,
Your name (Jesus) is ointment poured forth ....

Photo by Linda

The vitex chaste tree (Vitex agnus-castus) is a lovely, low-maintenance shrub that adds color, fragrance, and grace to the landscape. Most varieties of this ornamental plant grow between four to 15 feet tall and four to 12 feet wide, but some grow up to 30 feet tall and just as wide. The origin of this deciduous tree or shrub is Western Asia. (Wikipedia)

Last year, I bought this lovely tree. I had to fight two determined bumble bees to bring it home. In fact, we got home with one bee still in it.

In quiet meditation of Jesus and His life poured out for us, imagine this tree's fragrance like the presence of Jesus.

"Your name is like ointment poured forth."

John 12:3

*Then Mary took a pound of very costly oil of spikenard,
anointed the feet of Jesus, and wiped His feet (worship) with her hair.
And the house was filled with the fragrance of the oil.*

2 Corinthians 2:14

*Now thanks be to God who always leads us in triumph in Christ, and through
us diffuses the fragrance of His knowledge in every place.*

2 Corinthians 2:15

*For we are to God the fragrance of Christ among those who are being saved and
among those who are perishing.*

Blessings, and praise God from whom all blessings flow!

Self-Seeding Imitators of Christ

Bachelor Buttons

1 Corinthians 6:19-20

*Or do you not know that your body is the temple of the Holy Spirit
who is in you, whom you have from God, and you are not your own?
For you were bought at a price; therefore, glorify God in your body
and in your spirit, which are God's.*

Photo by Linda

Bachelor button (Centaurea cyanus) is a lightly fragrant, self-seeding wildflower native to Europe and Asia. Also known as cornflower, the most common variety boasts bright blue flowers and tall, sturdy stems. However, there are several varieties and unique cultivars with colors ranging from pink and white to purple and black. Depending on the variety, fully mature bachelor button plants can reach heights of three feet or more. Their petals are non-toxic and can be used as edible flowers in cooking or baking. (*Home & Life Style*—Ron Finley)

Our Bachelor Buttons are a very small variety which ranges from 4 to 6 inches tall. They are a bright spot in the garden. I wish I had more.

Because they are self-seeding, Batchelor Buttons remind me that as Christians, we should "be imitators of God as dear children" (Ephesians 5:1).

How can we call ourselves Christians if we do not read God's word and are not obedient to Him? As an imitator of Christ, we seek Christ's will in our associations, our belief's, our speech, our interactions with others, and especially NEVER, NEVER, NEVER humiliate, embarrass, or degrade our spouse. What happened to the phrase—honor, serve, and prefer? We are to be used by the Holy Spirit as self-seeding and non-toxic agents of God's love to others in a godless world.

Blessings, and praise God from whom all blessings flow!

God's Timing

Milkweed

Ecclesiastes 3:1-2

To everything there is a season, a time for every purpose under heaven:
A time to be born, And a time to die; a time to plant,
and a time to pluck what is planted ….

Photo by Linda

Milkweed, (genus Asclepias), genus of about 140 species of herbaceous perennial flowering plants belonging to the dogbane family. Milkweeds are found throughout North and South America. Many milkweed butterflies, including monarch butterflies, rely exclusively on milkweed plants as a food source for their larvae. These plants contain acrid milky juices that probably make the larvae and their subsequent stages distasteful to predators.

Most milkweeds have milky juice, flowers with five united petals, podlike fruits, and, usually, tufted seeds. Parts of the pollinia stick to visiting insect pollinators, which then carry them to other flowers to facilitate cross-pollination. This method of pollination is complex, but, when successful, the great numbers of pollen grains transferred result in the production of many seeds. The silky-haired seeds are drawn out of their pods by the wind and are carried off. (Britannica)

We have four of these plants, fitting the above description. Our milkweed is actually producing a silky translucent sack with enclosed seeds at this point.

The Plan of God's Salvation is Simple.

Romans 10:9

If you confess with your mouth the Lord Jesus and believe in your heart that God has raised Him from the dead, you will be saved.

However, the day by day walk with the Lord can be complex with interruptions. The milkweed is a simple, yet a complex plant that is dependent on God's timing for food for the butterflies and the cross-pollination of other plants.

We must determine to put God first in our daily time in the scriptures, our prayer life, and our time of praise and worship. Let the family and others know that your time with the Lord is essential and has top priority.

Acts 17:28

For in Him we live and move and have our being ….

We are God's special project and have been planted by the Lord (Psalm1:3) to share Christ's love and values to an ungodly culture. Just as the butterfly is dependent on the milkweed for food, we are dependent on God's word for our daily bread.

Be attentive to God's timing!!! Be attentive to God's ways and methods of sharing Christ! Be a cross-pollinator of God's love!

Blessings, and praise God from whom all blessings flow!

Seed the Love of Christ

Cleome

Matthew 28:18-20

And Jesus came and spoke to them, saying, "All authority has been given to Me in heaven and on earth. 19 Go therefore and make disciples of all the nations, baptizing them in the name of the Father and of the Son and of the Holy Spirit, 20 teaching them to observe all things that I have commanded you; and lo, I am with you always, even to the end of the age. Amen."

Photo by Linda

Cleome's (Cleomaceae) common names are cleomes, spider flower, Rocky Mountain bee plant, or stinking clover. It is an annual, ranging to 1.5 to 5 feet tall and 1 to 2 feet wide. It needs full to partial sun, average soil, well-drained, and acidic to neutral soil. Cleome is a summer flower that ranges in colors of white, pink, lavender, or rose. It is native to South America and does well in hardiness zones 10 and 11. This plant shrugs off pests and diseases and can self-seed excessively with seed pods that are long and pop open when ripe (Jamie Macintosh: for the magazine *The Spruce: Make Your Best Home*).

I just bought this weird plant. I wish that you could see the thin, long hairs in this picture. My only concern about this plant is that Texas may be too hot for it. We will see!

The seed pods are just like Christian evangelism. "Go you therefore ..." When we accept the Lord Jesus as our Savior, we want to tell others about His love and how He set us free from our sins. We become the seed pods on the Cleome plant. We grow and mature in Jesus and burst out—telling others of His mighty acts.

Psalm 145:4

One generation shall praise Your works to another,
And shall declare Your mighty acts.

Psalm150:2

Praise Him for His mighty acts; Praise Him
according to His excellent greatness!

Blessings, and praise God from whom all blessings flow!

The Passion Flower

Passiflora

Luke 23:34

*Then Jesus said, "Father, forgive them, for they do not know what they do."
And they divided His garments and cast lots.*

John 19:30

Jesus said, "It is finished!" And bowing His head, He gave up His spirit.

Photo by Linda

The Passion Flower (Passiflora spp.); Family: Passifloraceae; Common Names: Passionflower, Passion flower vine, Maypop, Granadilla is a perennial vine. At maturity, it can reach 10-30 feet tall and 3-6 feet wide. It can take full to partial sun and needs to be in a moist but well-drained soil either neutral or acidic.

This plant blooms only in summer, and has beautiful colors of purple blue, pink, red, or white. It is native to North America and South America and can live in hardiness zones 7-10 (www.thespruce.com/passion-flowers-1403114).

PASSION FLOWER is a woody vine that has unusual blossoms. Roman Catholic priests of the late 1500's named it for the Passion (suffering and death) of Jesus Christ. They believed that several parts of the plant, including the petals, rays, and sepals, symbolized features of the Passion. The flower's five petals and five petal-like sepals represented the 10 apostles who remained faithful to Jesus throughout the Passion. The circle of hair-like rays above the petals suggested the crown of thorns that Jesus wore on the day of His death. (AgriLife Extension: Texas A&M System)

Wow!!! How could I pass up a weird flower like this! I am thrilled that the Passiflora plant represents the Passion of our Savior, Jesus Christ.

> "When I survey the wondrous cross
> On which the Prince of glory died,
> My richest gain I count but loss,
> And pour contempt on all my pride.
>
> "Forbid it, Lord, that I should boast,
> Save in the death of Christ my God!
> All the vain things that charm me most,
> I sacrifice them to His blood.
>
> "See from His head, His hands, His feet,
> Sorrow and love flow mingled down!
> Did e'er such love and sorrow meet,
> Or thorns compose so rich a crown?

"Were the whole realm of nature mine,
That were a present far too small;
Love so amazing, so divine,
Demands my soul, my life, my all."

Isaac Watts

Blessings, and praise God from whom all blessings flow!

The Sweetness of Walking with Jesus

Psalm 19:9-10

The fear of the Lord is clean, enduring forever; the judgments of the Lord are true and righteous altogether. More to be desired are they than gold, Yea, than much fine gold; SWEETER also than honey and the honeycomb.

Ephesians 5:2

And walk in love, as Christ also has loved us and given Himself for us, an offering and a sacrifice to God for a sweet-smelling aroma.

Photo From Wikipedia

The Sweet Pea (Lathyrus odoratus; Family Fabaceae) flower's common name is Sweet Pea, perennial pea, everlasting pea. It is an annual vine that reaches the height of 6-8 feet tall. It needs full to partial sun in a well-drained alkaline soil. The bloom time is summer and fall with flower colors of red, pink, blue, white, and lavender. It is native to Europe and the Mediterranean areas. The hardiness zones are 3-8. This plant is toxic to humans and pets. www.thespruce.com/sweetpea

I have just planted the Sweet Pea seeds, and they have not yet grown. It may be too late in the summer for them to grow…but, I can hope. This flower reminds me of the "sweet smelling aroma" of our walk with Jesus!!!

I love God's Word! Jesus (THE WORD) is "clean," "enduring forever," "true and righteous," and I desire that fellowship and relationship more than riches.

I read God's Word!! I meditate on God's Word! I repent and confess my sins after reading God's Word!!! I pray God's Word! I sing God's Word!!! God's Word gives me a heart of gratitude and thankfulness!!! God's Word causes me to forgive and love people! God's Word gives me wisdom and direction!

Psalm 119:97

Oh, how I love Your law! It is my meditation all the day.

Blessings, and praise God from whom all blessings flow!

Precious Poppy

Romans 10:15

And how shall they preach unless they are sent? As it is written:
"How beautiful are the feet of those who preach the gospel of peace,
Who bring glad tidings of good things!"

Photo from Garden Therapy

The Poppy (Papaver somniferium) is beautiful. There are 10 types of poppy. Depending on the variety, it survives in hardiness zones 3-9. It needs full sun and moist, yet well-drained soil. At maturity it can reach 20-36 inches tall. The poppy is toxic to humans. Poppy flower colors range from white to vivid reds and oranges. There are cream, yellow, blue, and purple poppies as well.

Though found in the same genus as many popular garden poppies, you might want to steer clear of the opium poppy, from which heroin and other opiate drugs are derived. (Opium. Drug Enforcement Administration.) The opium poppy from Turkey has striking pink, red, purple, or white flowers; distinctive gray-green foliage; and is taller than most poppy flowers. By David Beaulieu www.thespruce.com/poppy

I have just planted some of these seeds. Hopefully, they will bloom.

This plant reminds me of how precious God's Word is.

However, God's Word is so much more meaningful when I think of the millions of men and women from the beginning of Christianity who have been tortured and killed as they shared God's "good news."

Romans 10:15

How beautiful are the feet of those who preach the gospel of peace,
Who bring glad tidings of good things!

Blessings, and praise God from whom all blessings flow!

Things I Learned from Our Garden

John 1:3 NLT

God created everything through him (Jesus), and nothing was created except through him.

Revelation 4:11 KJV

You are worthy, O Lord, to receive glory and honor and power: for you have created all things, and for your pleasure they are and were created.

Photos by Linda

Our Garden Revisited:

It has been a pleasure to take you on a tour of our garden. The Lord has demonstrated His great love, care, concern, and compassion to us as we have gazed upon His beautiful creations. All of the flowers are of different shapes, sizes, colors, water needs, and temperature challenges.

All of us were created with different gifts, talents, and temperaments by a wonderful, loving God so that we have fellowship with Him and explore His thoughts, ways, dreams, desires, plans, and purposes for our lives.

God has uniquely gifted you to reach someone for Christ, or to do something for the kingdom that others cannot do.

Dare to dream largely—outside of the box! What is in your heart to do? Have you dismissed it because it is too much work, or it seems impossible??? Are you a hermit—secretly wanting to do something, but afraid to step out in faith? Have you isolated yourself due to an inferiority complex, past hurts, or perhaps even lethargy?

Stop your stinking thinking! Look toward God! Listen to the call of the Master Creator! Repent! Take the first step in scripture meditation, scripture memorization, praise and worship, and prayer! Step into your dream or God's call upon you!

Nothing is impossible with God—regardless of your age or situation!

It is my sincere hope that you have enjoyed this walk through our garden with us.

Blessings, and praise God from whom all blessings flow!

Photos by Linda

About the Author

Asa E. Low Jr. was born in Dallas, Texas and grew up in Grand Prairie, Lewisville, and Flower Mound, Texas. He taught school for 41 years. He was active in church, serving as a deacon in Carrollton. From there, he became Headmaster at a Christian school in Dallas. He also served as associate pastor of two other churches. He taught choral music and music  theory at Mansfield High School in Mansfield, Texas, where he had a great impact on many students. After his retirement, Asa E. Low Jr. Intermediate School in Mansfield was named for him.

Asa and his wife of 56 years have four children and seven grandchildren.